L. U. Reavis

**The life and public services of Richard Yates, the war
governor of Illinois:**

A lecture delivered in the hall of the House of Representatives, Springfield,

Illinois, Tuesday evening, March 1st, 1881

L. U. Reavis

The life and public services of Richard Yates, the war governor of Illinois:
A lecture delivered in the hall of the House of Representatives, Springfield, Illinois,
Tuesday evening, March 1st, 1881

ISBN/EAN: 9783337732561

Printed in Europe, USA, Canada, Australia, Japan

Cover: Foto ©ninafisch / pixelio.de

More available books at **www.hansebooks.com**

THE

LIFE AND PUBLIC SERVICES

OF

RICHARD YATES

THE WAR GOVERNOR OF ILLINOIS.

A LECTURE

Delivered in the Hall of the House of Representatives, Springfield,
Illinois, Tuesday Evening, March 1st, 1881.

BY

HON. L. U. REAVIS.

You have earned the title of the "Soldier's Friend," and it is a title of nobility
of which you may well be satisfied. Your children will call it to mind with pleasure
when your earthly career shall have ended.—PROF. STURTEVANT.

ST. LOUIS, MO.:
PUBLISHED BY J. H. CHAMBERS & CO.
1881.

TO

HON. ENOS CLARKE,

A MEMBER OF THE ST. LOUIS BAR, ONE WHO HAS BEEN FROM TIME

TO TIME CALLED TO OFFICIAL STATION, AND WHO HAS BY HIS

LEARNING, FIDELITY AND KINDNESS BECOME WIDELY

ESTEEMED — ONE WHOSE EARLY MANHOOD

WAS DEVOTED TO THE GREAT PRIN-

CIPLES SO NOBLY SUSTAINED

BY THE SUBJECT OF

THIS ADDRESS,

THESE PAGES

ARE MOST RESPECTFULLY INSCRIBED BY

THE AUTHOR.

CORRESPONDENCE.

SPRINGFIELD, ILL., Jan. 24, 1881.

Hon. L. U. REAVIS, St. Louis, Mo:

DEAR SIR—Having learned that you have prepared a lecture upon the " Life, Character and Public Services of the Late ex-Governor and Senator Richard Yates," we take pleasure in requesting that you will deliver the same in Springfield at an early day, to be named by you.

Very respectfully yours,

S. M. CULLOM,	O. H. WRIGHT,
JOHN M. PALMER.	ORNAN PIERSON,
JOHN WILLIAMS,	JAMES G. WRIGHT,
JOHN M. HAMILTON,	J. M. GARLAND,
H. H. THOMAS,	JACOB WHEELER,
H. D. DEMENT.	JOHN MOSES,
CHAS. P. SWIGERT,	J. HENRY SHAW,
H. HILLIARD,	T. F. MITCHELL,
FRANK W. TRACY	ED. RUTZ,
JOHN W. PIERSON,	PAUL SELBY,
W. H. ALLEN,	W. M. SMITH,
L. C. COLLINS, Jr.	

ST. LOUIS, Mo., Jan. 25, 1881.

GENTLEMEN: I am in receipt of your communication of the 24th inst. inviting me to lecture on The Life and Public Services of the late Gov. Richard Yates. With many thanks I accept your invitation, and will, in the discharge of the engagement, meet you on the evening of Tuesday. March 1st, at Representatives' Hall.

In the hope that I may prove worthy the task you call me to perform, and that what I may say concerning the dead statesman will meet with the hearty approval of the people of Illinois, I am, with great respect, your obedient servant.

L. U. REAVIS.

His Excellency S. M. Cullom, Gen'l John M. Palmer, Hon. Jas. G. Wright and others.

The following resolution was unanimously adopted by the Illinois House of Representatives :

WHEREAS, The Hon. L. U. Reavis has been invited by the Governor and Lieutenant-Governor, the Speaker of the House, all the State officers and many other leading citizens, to deliver a lecture in this city on "The Life and Public Services of the late Governor and Senator Richard Yates," be it

Resolved, That the use of this hall be granted to Mr. Reavis, for next Tuesday evening, March 1, for the purpose of delivering said lecture.

At the conclusion of the lecture the following resolution, offered by Hon. Chas. T. Stratton, of Jefferson county, was adopted :

Resolved, That the thanks of this audience are hereby extended to Hon. L. U. Reavis, of St. Louis, Mo., for his eloquent review of the character, principles and life of the illustrious War Governor of our great State.

THE LIFE AND POLITICAL PRINCIPLES

—OF—

RICHARD YATES.

LADIES AND GENTLEMEN:

As a native of the State of Illinois, I am proud of her history. I delight to speak of the character and valorous deeds of her distinguished citizens, and to note her material, political and intellectual progress. This commonwealth has given more than its share of patriotism and greatness to the Republic. It possesses the population, wealth and material power of an empire, and it has within itself the undeveloped capacity of a great nation. Its rapid growth has no parallel in any of the States of the Union, and no man can set bounds to its future greatness.

The traditional and secular history of Illinois is enriched by the legends of the aborigines and the civic deeds of the adventurous Anglo-Saxon. A domain so distinctive in its physical character, so rich in productive power, and at once the primeval home and theater of mighty families of wild beasts and of nomadic savage tribes, long ago proclaimed its fitness to become the future home of civilized men having fixed habitations, government, learning, and of religion; the fixed energies of nature, the stupendous scenes of primeval activity, and the constantly accelerated growth of life from a condition of sensation up to conscious thought, were a perpetual prophecy of the future reign of law over this and conterminous territories, over which once ruled the good Hiawatha. The warm-hearted and zealous chieftain, who once led his band of savages to feasts and victories, has been succeeded by the intellectual and patriotic statesman; the wigwam has been changed to a palace, and the Indian village has been supplanted by the city of civilization, and to-day a new heaven and a new earth, is the inheritance of the American people.

As a physical section of our country, and as a political organism, the State of Illinois will ever remain one of the leading States in the American Union, and, as in the past, so in the future will her influence be great in the councils of the nation. Already the history of Illinois is made illustrious by the fame and patriotism of her distinguished citizens, inventors, manufacturers, teachers and statesmen. Such names as Williams, Strawn, Deere, McCormack, Funk, Sturtevant, Douglas, Lincoln, Grant, Yates and others, will forever stand as great land-marks in the history of this commonwealth.

Of these illustrious names I turn with solemn thoughts to that of Richard Yates, and in the warmth of my heart and the strength of my mind, speak concerning this gifted man of Illinois—this patriot of the Republic. At the name of Richard Yates, the people of Illinois love, adore and weep; they love the friend of their youth, of their children and their sacred homes; they adore the man who gave the full measure of his life to promote the happiness and well-being of his people, and to vindicate the supremacy of the federal constitution over all the States of the Republic. No children ever loved a fond parent better than the people of Illinois loved Richard Yates. His name was in every household, in every work-shop, and in every field of duty. It was but yesterday that he lived and moved among the living, a warm-hearted patriot, a devoted friend, and a great political teacher. To-day the grave of the dead statesman is still fresh in the necropolis. His deeds are all numbered, and, henceforth, he is to be judged with the same judgment wherewith we shall be judged. Since the close of the bloody scenes of the civil war, and since Richard Yates surrendered the physical to the spiritual and awoke into immortality, silence has reigned over his name. No storms of envy, no words of praise have disturbed his name since he was taken to his silent home. At the close of his earthly career, friends and opponents wept over the dead statesman, and turned from his burial place to the active scenes of life, almost forgetting that he ever lived. But his name remains a heritage for the living, and the history of his labors still endures with the freshness of an oriental tradition, like an eastern romance.

I come to this great State of Illinois, the home of Richard Yates, where he achieved so many victories of his ambition, to break the solemn silence of the tomb and call him forth, to be re-judged by living men and women, and to fix his name in history according to the measure of his labors and the influence of his earthly power. I enter upon the task with gratitude and emotions of warm filial love. I am a believer in hero worship as taught by Horace Greeley and Thomas Carlyle; and of the illustrious men whom I have known and admired in the days of their earthly glory, none did I ever admire more than Richard Yates.

The life of a nation is analogous to that of an individual; each has different and distinctive corresponding periods of development which succeed each other in the process of growth from youth to old age. The pioneer movement of the people of a nation is a period of national youth analogous to the life of the boy from childhood to the beginning of manhood. During the period of youth, the energies and individuality of the boy and the young nation are stimulated and strengthened for future usefulness and power according to the opportunities afforded. Not only is national life analogous to individual life, in the distinctive expression of each, but there is also an interblending of the life of the individual with the life of a nation—a psychological relation between the two which is expressed in the public life of each. The nation is wrought out of the habits and character of the people who create and administer it from generation to generation; so also do the inhabitants of a country derive many of their peculiarities of life, as individuals and communities, from the character of the country which they inhabit, and accordingly as nature expresses herself in the people, so do the people express themselves in the national life. If the country is full of the energies of nature, rich in productive power, vast in territorial extent, varied in its physical characteristics, and all nature is great and energetic, so will the inhabitants of the country be, and so will be the nation in its manifestations of life and its expressions of power. High altitudes bespeak an independent and liberty-loving people; vast plains tell of the abodes of honest and out-spoken people; rocks, mountains, rivers and forests generate great energy, individuality, strength of character, ambition, and aspiration. Our own country illustrates these truths: nature is great; our people are great and the Republic is great.

Thus far in our national career we have had little else but pioneer life. The blood of three generations flows in the veins of our people across the continent, from the Atlantic to the Pacific. The grand-parent upon the Atlantic seaboard greets the grand-child upon the Pacific shore, and each has lived in the wilderness of America, and contended with wild beasts and savages for the supremacy over nature. Soon after the organization of the government, the pioneer movement for the civil conquest of this continent began. From the home in the east, upon the Atlantic seashore, the hardy pioneer went forth to the western wilderness. The movement was conducted from Maine to Georgia with the precision of movement of a mighty army. Brave and hardy men and women, born in poverty and schooled in adversity, encouraged by tales told of the wilds of the west, went forth, pilgrims of empire, and in the simplicity of their modes of life, lived and loved in the wilderness of nature, and, as of old, begat sons and daughters. They moved in columns like armies to the field of battle—one column crossing the Susquehanna, another the Blue Ridge, and still other columns moving at other points, but all passing the defiles of the Appalachian Mountains and entering the States and Territories of the Valley of the Mississippi. The pioneer movement, once begun, continued to advance the outpost frontier line at an annual distance of twenty-two miles, until the Pacific ocean was reached. With the completion of the New York and Erie Canal, the central column, moving forward to the Mississippi River, was supported by a second column of pioneers moving to the northwest along the line of the great lakes and to the head waters of the Mississippi and Missouri Rivers. A third column moved and entered by the Gulf of Mexico, and occupied the region of the Southern States. Still another army of pioneers went around Cape Horn and across the Isthmus of Darien, and disembarked on the Pacific coast, and with all the lines closed in, the frontier armies completed the pioneer movement of the American people and accomplished the work of establishing an empire across the continent; and now we behold an empire of States, extending from ocean to ocean.

When this pioneer movement of the American people is fully and truly presented in history, it will stand forth as one of the most interesting and deeply significant events in all the annals of the world. It was the mightiest movement ever made by any people on this earth. This march of empire across the continent infinitely transcended the flight of the children of Israel from bondage. The exploration made by the Bedouin Arab, Abraham, pales before the exploration of Lewis and Clark.

Individual enterprise: the interests of communities: the aspirations of father and mother: the dictates of learning and law: the daring enterprise of Jesuit Fathers and the demonstrative spirit of religion, all united on the field of destiny and contributed to the onward movement of the great family of man, westward along the belt of empire. And the Star of Bethlehem, which arose in the East, on

" A gray morning by the sea,"

went down in Judea, and the star of empire arose in the West and became the pillar of fire by night, and the pillar of cloud by day, to direct the American pioneer in his westward career and herald to the world the coming of a new political dispensation destined to wrap the globe with its divine ordinances. This mighty pioneer movement of the American people—this movement that rocked the cradle for the future civilization of the world's people—gave to this country a race of western statesmen full of energy, originality and power. They were the offspring of a vigorous, sturdy and brave manhood and womanhood, that dared to confront the dangers and vicissitudes of the wilderness. Such men as Boone, Clark and Harney, were legitimate sons of the American pioneers. They were strong in native energies, courageous and enduring, and nature afforded no obstacle which they could not overcome. If the forests were to be felled, the mountains to be scaled, the rivers to be crossed, and savages and wild beasts to be subdued, such men as these with their native strength and inventive genius were always equal to the emergency.

Following in the footsteps of the earlier pioneers—the hunters, the Indian-fighters and explorers—came a race of robust statesmen, who, inspired with the spirit of liberty and progress, erected government over the wild domains of the great West, and laid the foundations of communities destined to bound forward in population, wealth and power. Business became organized, roads constructed, rivers bridged, manufactories established, farms improved, and education and religion were planted in the wilderness and fostered as higher exponents of the usefulness and mission of the human soul. And the boy, born in the wilderness in the log cabin, soon arose to distinction in society and State. With but a breath of time, and as if by the magician's wand, the wilderness of America has been transformed into fruitful fields and cities of civilization.

With the growth of population west of the Allegheny mountains, political power was organized, and Nashville, Tennessee, became the first great center of political power in the West. A bright constellation of fearless men clustered around the capital of Tennessee; men, whose eloquence, abilities and statesmanship exerted a powerful influence in all parts of the country, and especially in the federal metropolis. Conspicuous in this constellation of representative men were Jackson, Polk, Grundy, Bell, Jones, Houston and Payton.

At the time these men were in active public life there was no other association of men, west of the Allegheny mountains, equal to them in ability, and in the strong and demonstrative character of their lives. They were giants in the land, the scope of whose labors were national, and they laid deep and broad the foundations of Western Empire. Decades passed away, and immigration from the States south of the Ohio River and from New England began to move to the north-western country, and with the growth of that region, political power passed from Tennessee; Springfield, Illinois, became the successor of Nashville, and the center of a more brilliant, a more illustrious constellation of distinguished statesmen. They were the sons of hardy pioneers, most of them seeking the freedom of the State of Illinois as a refuge from a land of bondage. Some were young men from the East seeking homes in the great West. Those most distinguished in this constellation of giant statesmen were Lincoln, Douglas, Trumbull, Dillon, Breese, Hardin, Baker, Gillespie, Browning, Shields, Richardson, Yates, Logan and Palmer. Most of these men were born in the log-cabins of the wilderness, and from that humble birthplace arose to the highest stations in our political society. Some of them have distinguished themselves on battle fields; some on the judge's bench; some in the legislative halls and the executive chair of this State; and still others in the legislative halls and the executive chair of the nation. But all were patriotic and illustrious men—all great landmarks in State and National history—and all have impressed their principles on the institutions of our common country.

You will observe that in this constellation of distinguished men is the name of the patriotic war-governor of Illinois. His brilliancy in this galaxy of statesmen is like that of a star in the heavens, that evolves its own light. He, too, evolved his own light from his own brilliant mind.

Richard Yates was born in the little village of Warsaw, in Gallatin county, Kentucky, January 18th, 1815. His ancestors were of English origin. The family name is very common at this time in many parts of England, and especially are the Yateses very numerous in Liverpool and Manchester, where they rank high in English society. Several generations ago the ancestors of Richard Yates migrated from England to Virginia, where they settled and became engrafted into the American stock. His parents moved from Virginia to Kentucky, and there at a very early time the transplanted stock germinated in a new and broader field of human activity and human destiny. At the time of the birth of Richard Yates, the population of Kentucky was but little more than 500,000, and the population of the entire country was but little more than 9,000,000. Then there were but twenty-one States in the Federal Union. But the child was born under the ægis of liberty — born in a land foreseen by the inspired Seneca, long before Columbus sailed through the gates of the sea to discover the New World. The stock from whence Richard Yates sprang, was of superior blood; a family vigorous, healthy, industrious, and ambitious. His father and mother were gifted and noble by nature. They were generous in a high degree, and broad in the executive duties and administration of their family affairs. Richard was born in a log cabin. He was cradled in the wilderness; and his mother wispered in his infant ears, tales of the Indian war-whoop, which was common to her early settlement in Kentucky. His mother taught him royal lessons of fidelity and loyalty, and awakened in his young mind aspirations for greatness, which took deep root in the young mind, and blossomed and fruited in manhood's prime.

Born in the log cabin. Let me stop at this word—this birth-place, this palace of a stalwart army of the great men of America. The log-cabin! I turn back through a period of only sixty years, and look across the Ohio River. There, in the days gone by, stood, upon the other shore of that river, the log cabin, the birth-place of Richard Yates, the future Governor of Illinois, and one of the nation's great patriots and statesmen. I go further back in the years gone by, and in Hardin county, Kentucky,

I see another log cabin standing alone in the wilderness, with narrow limits and without adornment, and this is the birth-place of Abraham Lincoln, the weird child of the forest, the future law-giver and the future President of the Republic. He came forth from the log cabin like the man from Bozrah whose garments were dyed in blood. Never did mortal man walk the earth with such grandeur. He was the giant of the forest home —the cyclopean head of the Republic. He became the political teacher of the people and the Moses and law-giver of the nation. I go still further back in the years gone by, and in the wilds of Virginia I see another log cabin, the birth-place and home of Henry Clay, the great commoner of the American people—the inspired statesman, the great political leader. Coeval with Clay was Jackson, also born in a log cabin in North Carolina, and a typical American. As a friend, loving and magnanimous ; as an enemy, brave and terrible ; without learning and without genius, but with an enormous amount of that uncommon thing called common sense, which enabled him to do the right thing at the right time. Successful alike as the leader of an army, or of a nation, Jackson began in a log cabin and ended in the White House. I sweep the history of my country and I find in the generations gone by, children born in the log cabin, and reared in orphanage and in the most trying adversity, rising to the highest stations in life ; some engaging in the profession of arms, others in the professions of law, medicine and divinity, and still others leading in the great commercial and industrial pursuits of the country. The log cabin is the birth-place of heroic life, of sovereign manhood and womanhood. It is the citadel of virtue, the high-walled fortress of public motherhood and parental devotion. It has done for America that which the palace could not do. It has produced the most wonderful galaxy of legislators, jurists, soldiers and rulers that ever enriched history. None of the poisonous influences of rank and cancerous society ever besieged the log cabin to lead astray the children of the forest and plain. Schooled in the simple habits of the wilderness, and constantly drawing fresh life from nature, the child of the log cabin is fated to be strong in physical and mental power and self-reliant in the conflicts of life.

In the vicinity of the log cabin stood the school house, in which the boy of the log cabin drank into his soul more inspiring lessons of divine life than ever came from Grecian oracle

or Pierian spring. I would not say aught against our great in
stitutions of learning, and the refining influences of our civilization, but there is something wrong in our social order—in the
present tendency of our society. Survey the institutions of the
country; look to the three learned professions; look to the
birth-place of the children of the Republic—where do you find
in the parental home of to-day the vigorous, industrious, brave
and high-spirited mothers, such as of yore? Where can you
find the sons,

"Such as the Doric mothers bore,"

—sons into whose manly capabilities the government of the
Republic can be committed with safety and honor? Traverse the
country from centre to circumference and where can you find
a nobler American manhood than of yore? Where are they who
are waiting to teach and lead the age in which we live? Where
are to be found the scholars, students and teachers equal to
those of one, two and three generations ago? Where shall we
go to find political leaders, teachers and law-givers equal to
those born in the log cabin? I assert that there is a flagrant
weakness pervading our entire people and our social condition.
Nowhere exists that strong and embracing self-hood—that
bravery, energy, will-power and determination—among our
people, for which they were noted in the generations past. If
you ask, What is the matter? I answer: That the energies, the
industry, the moral strength, the manhood and womanhood and
virtue of the people, have gone out through the base-ball clubs,
through fashionable watering places, through the theatres and
novel reading, through rum-shops and woman-suffrage agita
tions, and other modern creations and mercenary tendencies of
our people. Not under such influences, but under far different
influences were produced our Websters and Calhouns; our
Gaineses and Scotts; our Richeys and Greeleys.

Henry Yates, the father of Richard, though limited in education, was a man endowed with superior excellencies of mental-
ity, character and manhood, and wherever he was known he
was noted for his broad and generous expressions of wisdom in
all the affairs of life. He was at once a teacher and a leader in
the community in which he lived. Endowed by nature with the
principles of true humanity, he recognized the rights of all and

the freedom of all. He hated human slavery, and from the slave State of Kentucky he looked across the Ohio to the promised land of Illinois, in the hope of better years. With his family he moved in 1831 to Springfield, Illinois, where he located and engaged in the mercantile business. In this and in a neighboring locality he remained until his death. Richard was sent to school to Illinois College, and graduated in 1837. He was one of the first graduates of that institution, and gave bright promise of future usefulness and distinction. He immediately entered the law office of Col. John J. Hardin, one of the most brilliant and highly esteemed men of the West, with whom he acquired the profession of law; but his ambition urged him to wider fields of duty in other fields of distinction. In early life, in very boyhood, the soul of Richard Yates was fired with an ardent ambition—an ambition for fame and greatness which unconsciously knocks at the door of the understanding of the child of destiny, and tells of a shining future; an ambition which, like the Amruta cup of Indian fable, gives to the corrupt and the bad a life of misery; but to the virtuous and the good, a life of everlasting glory. The child of destiny feels in early youth a yearning for greatness, and that repressed yearning cannot be satisfied by the sneers of ignorant nor by the embarrassments of poverty. And although the child of destiny dare not, for fear of scorn, reveal to his associates the aspirations of his soul, he walks forth, encouraged by the conscious strength of his own selfhood, and communes with nature; learns lessons from running brooks, from hill and plain, and drinks inspiration from the breezes; and confiding in his own destiny, he looks to the stars, and his mind illuminated by the influxes of wisdom from above, reads his own royal future in the riper years of life.

Edgeworth tells us that fame sometimes gives her votaries visions of their future destiny while yet in early life. There is then a sort of sympathy created between their youthful aspirations and coming deeds—a reflection of the future upon the present.

In his very boyhood he walked a distance of twelve miles to hear a speech from Henry Clay, and with self-conscious majesty he walked into the reception-parlor where Mr. Clay was receiving his friends, and presented himself as one of them. The great statesman took young Yates by the hand and spoke a few kind words, and told him to be seated. Mr. Clay knew the father of young Yates, and in the greatness of his nature extended his friendship and sympathies to the boy whose ambition it was to link himself to the great man in whose footsteps he aspired to walk, and whose greatness he desired to emulate. Mr. Clay extended to young Yates the friendship of a sage, and took him to dinner, and to the speaker's stand, and in thus doing impressed upon the young mind of Richard the first great lesson of ambition. From thenceforth Richard Yates went forward to the duties of life with an unconquerable determination to achieve honor and distinction among his fellows, and to write his name high upon the scroll of fame. No allurements in the path of life, no temptations of wealth, diverted his attention from this single aim—this fixed purpose to achieve political greatness ; and thus directing his efforts, he became a member of the Illinois Legislature in 1842, being then twenty four years of age. He was elected successively for six years. He distinguished himself as a member by his marked ability, and his efforts to procure legislation for the promotion of the general good of the State; to aid in the building of asylums, institutions of learning and public improvements essential to the material advancement of the commonwealth of Illinois. In this field of duty he early demonstrated himself to be a magnanimous and public-spirited man.

It was in the Legislature of Illinois that Richard Yates first attacked slavery. He was by nature a believer in human rights and human liberty, and a determined opponent of slavery.

In party politics he was a Whig, and in 1850 he was nominated and elected to Congress by the Whigs. On entering the national legislature he found himself to be the youngest member in the House of Representatives. But with that same self-conscious majesty which was a part of his nature, he entered the field of national politics, undaunted by a consciousness of youth, and unhesitating for the want of experience. In Congress he rapidly grew into favor with public men. His courteous and amiable demeanor won universal esteem. When he was re elected to Congress in 1852, party leaders and distinguished men in all ranks of life universally and instinctively foresaw the coming of a great political crisis. The Whig party exhausted all its power in the presidential contest of 1852, to wrest the country from the hands of the Democratic party.

Failing to elect General Scott, and seeing the growing obstinacy of the pro-slavery party on one side, and the growing determination of the anti-slavery party on the other side, the Whig party dissolved its organization. It had always been devoted to the maintenance of the law, though opposed to the extension of slavery. The presidential contest of 1852 demonstrated a growing tendency toward two extreme conditions of political society, a growing tendency in the pro-slavery wing of the Democratic party to extend slavery and make it national instead of sectional; on the other hand a growing tendency on the part of the anti-slavery men to resist the further spread of slavery, even to the trampling down of national law. The Whig party was powerless to arrest the extreme and sectional tendencies. A great political contest was precipitated upon the country. In the inauguration of that contest Richard Yates was a participant. He was the only member of Congress from Illinois, down to 1854, who raised his voice in favor of freedom in Kansas. His speech against the passage of the Nebraska bill was one of the best efforts of his life, and fully demonstrated the higher conviction of his mind, the real man that he was. He entered the great contest in the vigor of manhood, and with the ardor of an enthusiast. His birth, and that of his parents, in a slave State, contributed to strengthen his opposition to human slavery, and stimulate him to vindicate the cause of human freedom. Born and educated in the principles of the Whig party, he was the friend and supporter of law and order, the defender and promoter of dignified and honorable party contests.

At the death of the Whig party the Republican party was organized with the avowed purpose of resisting the spread of slavery. It was essentially an anti-slavery party. It embodied in its organization the great mass of active thinking and progressive people of the country. It was a progressive and aggressive party. And with a far-reaching and comprehensive spirit of progress the Republican party encouraged education and gave its support to the material improvement of the country. The Democratic party, loaded with incrusted institutionalism, and trusting in boundless confidence, on the dictation and authority of its precedents, angrily insisted that its political right to power should not be questioned and that its rule should not be subverted. The parties being thus arrayed in thought and conventionality against each other, the great conflict between slavery and freedom was waged. The State of Illinois was under the control of the Democratic party, and was re-districted for the purpose of securing a Democratic member of Congress in the place of Yates. This end was accomplished and he was defeated for Congress in 1854. But as true as the needle to the pole, was he to his faith in political freedom. When his defeat was ascertained in 1854, he fearlessly and distinctively announced to the public that by the very principles on which he went down, he would in the future rise more glorious and triumphant.

On his return to private life he engaged in business in the construction of a railway through the central portion of the State of Illinois. As president of the company he demonstrated unusual ability in the prosecution of the work.

But not content with the honors and emoluments of business in private life, and not satisfied with being a simple looker-on amid the threatening and bitter contests of a gigantic political struggle, Richard Yates entered the Presidential campaign of 1856. His heart, soul, mind and strength were with the Republican party. The struggle in Kansas had gone on; freedom and slavery had met face to face on the plains of that virgin territory. On the one side was progressive thought; on the other side, audacious and bigoted institutionalism, that scorned at the questionings of political and intellectual progress. The contest went on; it had assumed a sectional aspect, and the best thought of the North and the South was brought into fierce conflict.

The Presidential contest of 1856 was a contest between slavery and freedom. The result demonstrated that the capital invested in slave property and the political convictions of more than two generations could not be hastily overthrown, and the Democratic party secured another lease of political power under James Buchanan, and the bitterness of the contest stimulated that party to the execution of measures still more aggressive in favor of the spread of slavery. The Dred Scott decision came declaring the privilege of the use of negro property universal under the Constitution. This decision was soon followed by President Buchanan's letter to Prof. Silliman, of Yale College, declaring that the right to take slave property into the territories was unquestioned by the Constitution. The pro-slavery party, acting wholly through the Democratic party, having announced their principles and politics as being justified and guaranteed by precedents and law, barricaded itself under the feudal forms of institutionalism. On the other hand, the exponents of the anti-slavery party — the leaders of the new Republican party —sought to enthrone themselves upon the doctrines of the HIGHER LAW. At this time the issue between freedom and slavery was clearly defined. The Democratic party rested the cause of slavery upon precedent, law, institutionalism, and an extraordinary interpretation of the Constitution. The Republican party held that slavery was wrong — a social cancer, and a tyrant, which deprived human beings of their inalienable rights and retarded the advancement of civilization. The issues were made broad, and were deeply rooted in the convictions of those who assumed to defend on either side. On one side was intrenched the infamous and audacious authority of so-called institutional infallibility; on the other side, was rapidly being developed and consecrated, the conscience of enlightened mankind. The great Channing had given the strength of his mind. against slavery and class legislation. Charles Sumner, in 1854, and in the spirit of moderation, warned the South of the coming contest. Said Sumner: " As long as my actions or utterances are inspired by the obligation of an oath under the law, I will never do aught, or counsel to disturb or interfere with the rights of your peculiar institution; but I tell you now, and I offer no apology for telling you, that ere long the very great wrongs suffered by the millions you control, will be suppressed by the voice of an enlightened public sentiment, not, I hope, the voice of a section, but the harmonious response to the dictation of our Creator."

Victor Hugo, the most divinely gifted man of our planet, declared American slavery to be the greatest moral deformity of the nineteenth century. Theodore Parker enunciated a new Golden Rule, defining the law of right between the freeman and the slave. It was not so broad in its scope and expression of human conduct as the dual Golden Rule enunciated by Confucius, or so fresh in its expression of the principle of humanity, as the rule enunciated by Jesus of Nazareth, but it taught that what a man had the right to do for himself, his neighbor had the right to aid him to do.

North and South the battle raged; the sharp conflicts of mind on fundamental principles of human rights, produced more mobs in Boston than elsewhere in the country. Southern aristocracy arrayed itself against the Democratic spirit of the people, and the laborers of the North were denominated mud-sills, greasy mechanics, and small-fisted farmers. Crimination was answered on both sides by re-crimination, without reason or wisdom. Kansas became a political battle-ground. On that Western territory, the North and the South in their representatives and constituents, submitted their issues to the will of the people. The struggle in Kansas formed an epoch in the political history of the Republic, and the result of the struggle heralded a new dispensation of civil liberty to mankind.

Party contests were bitter in Kansas: the denunciation of party leaders was outspoken. At the Republican State Convention of Illinois, held at Bloomington, 1856, in a speech made by Richard Yates, he said: "At the names of Atchison and Stringfellow the mothers of Kansas press their babes to their bosoms!" In the contest in Kansas, one party known as "Border Ruffians," and another as "Carpet-baggers, sent out by the New England Emigrant Aid Society." On both sides, partisan strife overshadowed all conception of inter-state citizenship, and stimulated bitter contention between the slave and free States—between the North and the South. This contention constantly intensified until the Presidential contest of 1860, when another appeal was made to the people to determine upon the principles of the two parties. The leaders of the Republican party were able and united. In the main, they were the best and most distinguished men from the Whig and Democratic parties. They entered the political struggle of 1860 with earnestness and determination, and, as a sectional party, representing the sentiment of the North, they controlled a majority of the voters of the North. The Democratic party was divided from the beginning. The division which took place at the Charleston convention was never healed, and the republican party entered the contest against three other tickets, and with Yancy and others bitterly opposing the election of either ticket.

The Republican party of Illinois met in convention at Decatur in May, 1860, and nominated Richard Yates for Governor. His nomination was regarded the best that could have been made, because he embodied the golden mean of the Republicans of Illinois. With Abraham Lincoln at the head of the national ticket, and Richard Yates at the head of the State ticket, Illinois be came the theater of intense and exasperated political strife. The candidacy of Douglas virtually contributed to the election of Lincoln to the presidency, and the political faith of Illinois being founded upon the ordinance of 1787, stimulated her people to cast their majority vote for the Republican ticket. The candidacy of Bell and Everett was not founded upon a single living political principle, and only served as an obsolete, effete political altar, on which aged and expiring politicians could sacrifice themselves for the pretended good of their country. The campaign of 1860 brought into recognition the intellectual and moral power of the North; for, with the people of the North, the vital issue was founded upon a great question of human rights. In fact, the contest was a struggle between two antagonistic forms of political society — between slavery and freedom. Slavery had constantly menaced the permanency of the government since the enunciation of the Declaration of Independence, and, from time to time, freedom yielded to its requests, until the intellectual and moral growth of the American people became so strong and determined as to demand that slavery be checked in its career, and, like other crimes, be hedged in by the law of the nation. This demand of freedom was granted by the American people, according to the forms of law, in 1860, by the election of Abraham Lincoln to the presidency of the United States. The central idea and aim running through all the political teachings of Mr. Lincoln was in favor of the extension and application to political society of freedom and the doctrines of the Declaration of Independence. Nevertheless, he was by nature a conservative man, and, by education, a rigid adherent and supporter of the law. But his election was made a pretext for secession by those to whom defeat threatened change, and to whom change threatened injury; and embittered by prejudices and the party strife of many years, and maddened by defeat, the people of the Cotton States declined to acquiesce in the election of Abraham Lincoln, and planting themselves upon the doctrine of State Rights, entered upon the work of secession — a calamity which the founders of the Republic and all succeeding patriots earnestly sought to avert. Before the inauguration of Mr. Lincoln, the work of secession was far under way. The inefficiency and indifference of President Buchanan, about enforcing the authority of the Constitution over the domain of the South, caused his cabinet to be dismembered, and the old Ship of State was left to the mercy of the wind and waves of rebellion. In after years, when the Republic has passed into the hands of other generations soon to follow, the administration of James Buchanan will be inscribed in our country's history as a confirmation of a great poetic truth:

" Wrong forever on the throne ;
Right forever on the scaffold ;
But that scaffold sways the future,
And behind the dim unknown
Standeth God, within the shadow,
Keeping watch above his own."

On assuming the office of Chief Executive of the nation, President Lincoln was called upon, *at once,* to confront a gigantic war between the States of the North and the South. Siege was levied against Fort Sumter, and hostile armies were being organized to resist the authority of the supreme law of the Government. By the obligations of the oath of office, Lincoln was compelled to use all the power of the nation to put down this wanton and criminal defiance of law, this treasonable assault on the life of the nation. Before his inauguration, nearly every State of the North was provided with a new and patriotic Governor, ready to bring into requisition the full power of their respective States to subordinate the insurgents to the will of the Union. One of the most conspicuous, patriotic and brave of the loyal Governors of the North was Richard Yates. He had already taken the oath of office and assumed the executive chair of Illinois. He fully comprehended the threatening contest before Lincoln had reached the executive mansion of the nation. In this approaching revolution, the home of Lincoln and the stronghold of Republicanism, Illinois, was looked upon as the great and growing central State of the West, and all eyes were turned to the Governor of the great commonwealth. Loyal men in Missouri, Kentucky and other neighboring States looked to Illinois and to Governor Yates as the boon and center of patriotism and power in the Valley of the Mississippi. They looked to it to rally first to the support of Abraham Lincoln in the defense and maintenance of the government. Richard Yates had already won for himself a national reputation as an able exponent of the principles of the Republican party, and, as the Chief Executive of Illinois, his position before the people of the West and the country, was regarded as being pre-eminent. On the

assembling of the legislature, in January, 1861, and some months
before fire opened on Fort Sumter, in his inaugural message,
Governor Yates announced himself firm, clear and patriotic in
the expression of his views concerning the cause of the Union,
and the determination of Illinois to vindicate the supremacy of
the Constitution in the coming contest.

"Referring to the national affairs," said Governor Yates: "whatever
may have been the divisions of parties hitherto, the people of Illinois will,
with one accord, give their assent and firm support to two propositions.
First. That obedience to the Constitution and the laws must be insisted upon
and enforced, as necessary to the existence of the Government. *Second.* That
an election of Chief Magistrate of the nation, in strict conformity with the
Constitution, is no sufficient cause for the release of any State from any of its
obligations to the Union."

A minority of the people may be persuaded that a great error has been
committed by such election, but for relief in such a contingency, the Constitution looks to the efficacy of frequent elections, and has placed it in the
power of the people to remove their agents and servants at will. The work-
ing of our government is based upon the principles of the indisputable
rights of majorities. To deny the right of those, who have constitutionally
succeeded by ballot to stations only to be occupied, is not merely unfair and
unjust, but revolutionary; and for a party which has constitutionally tri-
umphed, to surrender the powers it has won, would be an ignoble submission,
a degradation of manhood, a base desertion of the people's service, which
should inevitably consign it to the scorn of Christendom and the infamy of
history.

To give shape and form to their purpose of resistance, the dissatisfied
leaders of the South Carolina movement have revived the doctrine long since
exploded, that a State may nullify a law of Congress and secede from the
Union at pleasure. Such a doctrine can never for a moment be permitted.
Its admission would be fatal to the existence of government, would dissolve
all the relations which bind the people together, and reduce to anarchy the
order of the Republic.

This is a government entered into by the people of the whole country in
their sovereign capacity, and although it have the sanction also, of a compact
between sovereign States, does not receive its chief support from that cir-
cumstance, but from the original and higher action of the people themselves.

This Union cannot be dissolved by one State, nor by the people of one
State or of a dozen States. This government was designed to be perpetual
and can be dissolved only by revolution.

Secession is disunion. Concede to South Carolina the right to release her
people from the duties and obligations belonging to their citizenship, and
you annihilate the sovereignty of the Union by prostrating its ability to
secure allegiance. Could a government which could not vindicate itself, and
which had exhibited such a sign of weakness, command respect or long
maintain itself? If that State secede, why may not California and Oregon,

and with better reason, because they are remote from the Capital, and separated by uninhabited wildernesses and vast mountain ranges, and may have an independent commerce with the shores and islands of the Pacific and the marts of the Indies? Why may not Pennsylvania secede and dispute our passage to the seaboard through her territory? Why may not Louisiana constitute herself an independent nation, and dictate to the people of the great Northwest the onerous terms upon which their millions of agricultural and industrial products might find a transit through the Mississippi and be delivered to the commerce of the world.

It will be admitted that the territory of Louisiana, acquired in 1803, for the purpose of securing to the people of the United States the free navigation of the Mississippi, could never had seceded; yet it is pretended, that when that territory has so perfected its municipal organization as to be admitted into the Union as a State, with the powers and privileges equal to the other States, she may at pleasure repudiate the union, and forbid to the other States the free navigation which was purchased at the cost of all, not for Louisiana, but for all the people of the United States. A claim so presumptuous and absurd could never be acquiesced in. The blood of the gallant sons of Kentucky and Tennessee was freely shed to defend New Orleans and the Mississippi River from a foreign foe ; and it is memorable that the chieftain who rescued that city from sack and siege, was the same, who at a later date by his stern and patriotic rebuke, dispersed the ranks of disunionists in the borders of South Carolina.

Can it be for a moment supposed that the people of the Valley of the Mississippi, will ever consent that the great river shall flow for hundreds of miles through a foreign jurisdiction, and they be compelled—if not to fight their way in the face of the forts frowning upon its banks—to submit to the imposition, annoyance of arbitrary taxes and exorbitant duties to be levied upon their commerce? I believe that before that day shall come, either shore of the " Father of Waters " will be a continuous sepulchre of the slain, and with all its cities in ruins, and the cultivated fields upon its sloping sides laid waste, it shall roll its foaming tide in solitary grandeur, as at the dawn of creation. I know I speak for Illinois, and I believe for the Northwest, when I declare them as a unit in the unalterable determination of their millions occupying the great basin drained by the Mississippi, to permit no portion of that stream to be controlled by a foreign jurisdiction.

I believe and trust it is to be the mission of those to whom the people have lately committed, for a period, the interests of this nation, to administer public affairs upon the theory of THE PERPETUITY OF THE CONSTITUTION AND THE GOVERNMENT ORGANIZED UNDER IT.

No matter how vociferously South Carolina may declare that the Union is dissolved, and that she and other States are out of the Confederacy, no recognition whatever is due to her self-assumed independence in this regard. It took seven years to establish our independence. The precious boon purchased by patriot blood and treasure was committed to us for enjoyment, and to be transmitted to our posterity, with the most solemn injunctions that man has the power to lay on man. By the grace of God we will be faithful to the trust. For seven years yet to come, at least, will we struggle to maintain a perfect Union—a government of one people, in one nation, under one Constitution.

It is, perhaps, impossible to tell what may be the exact result of this South Carolina nullification, but do what she will, conspire with many or few, I am confident that this Union of our fathers—a Union of intelligence, of freedom, of justice, of industry, of religion, of science and art, will, in the end, be stronger and richer and more glorious, renowned and free, than it has ever been heretofore, by the necessary reaction of the crisis through which we are passing.

In proclaiming these fundamental doctrines of constitutional government, Gov. Yates demonstrated to the world that he comprehended three great underlying truths of vital concern to the people of this country and the government under which they live.

First, that this is a nation, and not a league of states associated by common consent, with the right of withdrawing from the compact at will.

The doctrine of Secession is the political infidelity of the world. It resists all supreme authority, denies the existence of an overruling law, and leaves petty communities at the mercy of all political isms, and provides no restraint against treason. All along the highway of time the governments of the world have been prematurely destroyed by the same doctrine of Secession which has threatened the destruction of this Republic. The city states of the middle ages were founded and destroyed by this same South Carolina heresy, and as long as it has an advocate and a friend in this country it will menace the permanency of this Union.

We are one people, made so by the war for national independence and the war for the Union; and it is a monstrous blunder, a gigantic heresy, to teach that secession is liberty, and that constitutional law is centralization. If any man entertains the heresy of secession, let me tell him that there is no liberty but the liberty of law, and there is no government but the government of law. License is not liberty. It is the rule of action for the mob and the savage. Territory purchased by the people of the United States and clothed with a State government and admitted into the Union, cannot, in the very nature of things, become greater than the Union, and, therefore, must be subject to the rule of the Constitution. In no way does the new State retain the lawful right in itself to withdraw from the Union at will; hence the absurdity of a State assuming authority in violation of the Constitution.

Our emblems of government point to the sovereignty of the Constitution over all the States. The flag is a national emblem. The great seal of the government is a national emblem. So, too, is the stamp upon the money of the government.

If we turn to behold the benefits growing out of the influence of sovereign political convictions, on the one hand, and the convictions of secession, on the other hand, how sad is the contrast! On one side we see the national expression in favor of a general system of education, of loyalty, population, wealth and power. On the other side, where the doctrine of secession prevails, we find education and enterprise languishing, and the children of great States that ought to be prosperous and powerful, growing up without culture and without hope.

A second fundamental truth comprehended and enunciated by Gov. Yates in his inaugural message is, that the Mississippi valley must forever remain the political home of one people, of one nation ; and that as long as the mighty Mississippi river extends through this valley, from zone to zone and from climate to climate, but one people will drink of its waters from north to south. That river, in itself, is a stronger bond of political union than the Constitution, and with a grasp of mind like that of Scott and Benton, Gov. Yates boldly announced this great fundamental truth.

This grand valley is to be the perpetual home of industry, of wealth and political power. Here will be enacted the great contests in labor and civilization, in law and social order, for here will grow the dense masses of population who will be compelled to engage in the industrial pursuits. On the slopes of the continent will grow a less dense population, with a higher civilization and a superior æsthetic life.

Perhaps in no way did the American people present a stronger expression of the value of hardy manhood during the civil war than that marked demonstration of power in the valley of the Mississippi. When the struggle commenced, Gen. Scott commanded the army ; Gen. Dix, of New York, commanded that department; Gen. Butler, of Massachusetts, commanded in Baltimore; Gen. McClellan, of New York, commanded the department of Ohio, and Gen. Lyon, of Connecticut, the department of Missouri—all Eastern men. When the war closed, Gen. Grant,

of Illinois, was at the head of the Army; General Sherman, of
Missouri, had brought his Western army into North Carolina;
General Thomas, of Ohio, had command in Tennessee, and
General Sheridan, of Ohio, was Grant's favorite subordinate in
the army before Richmond—all Western men.
A third fundamental truth enunciated by Gov. Yates in his
inaugural message, was, that the great struggle which was then
impending would redeem the nation from the blight of slavery,
and make her stronger, richer and more glorious by the
necessary reaction of the crisis through which she was destined to pass.

Already we have unlimited evidence of the truth of this
conception, and this truth is confirmed by the boundless confidence which the people have in the future. In the language of
Horace Greeley, " When fire opened upon Fort Sumter, notice
was given to the world that the era of diplomacy and com-
promise had ended." The long-threatened contest between the
North and South had at last come, and the appeal was made,
through the forms of law to the loyal people of the country
to rally in the defense of the Constitution and the Union. At
the call of the Washington Government hundreds of thousands
rushed to the rescue of the national life, and to the subordina-
tion of the slave States to the will of the Union. At this criti-
cal period, when no man could tell to what magnitude the
rebellion would grow, or to what end it would lead, Gov. Yates
was found equal to the task entrusted to him by the people of
Illinois. He rose in full official power and personal grandeur
to a full comprehension of the great crisis, and demonstrated
his equal ability to discharge his whole duty, as executive of
the great State of Illinois. His devotion to free government,
his aspirations for national greatness, and his undying devotion
to the Union of these States, contributed to make him the
most fit man of all the political leaders in Illinois, for chief
executive, at the time of the great crisis of the rebellion. He
entered upon the discharge of his official duties at a time when
to be conservative was to be wrong, when to be right was to be
revolutionary. He sent forth, to make battle against the
enemy, a loyal army more powerful than was ever led by Ses-
ostris, Alexander, Cæsar or Charlemagne. The loyal men of
Illinois went not to fight for Pagan or Imperial conquests; they
went to compel insurgents to stand by the contract entered

into for the establishment of the Government of the United
States, by " we, the people." The sequel proved the contract
to be valid, and its binding force unalterable by any part of
the contractors.

Gov. Yates grew with the contest in all its gigantic propor-
tions and its fierce conflicts, until he became the personal embodiment of the great State of Illinois. Emerson tells us that
Plato is philosophy and philosophy is Plato. In the magnitude of his great and beneficent personality, and in the fullness
of official power as Governor, Yates was Illinois and Illinois
was Yates. He was earnest, decisive, courageous and persis-
tent in his efforts to put down the rebellion, and withal, he was
gifted and guided in his efforts by a superabundance of practi-
cal wisdom. Stupendous preparations for war were hastily
executed on either side, and public men, and those in the private walks of life, were rapidly taking sides in the contest. In
this crisis of the nation's life, Douglas lost no time in announc-
ing to the country on which side he stood; and after thorough
consultations in Washington with President Lincoln and other
leaders, he returned to the Capital of Illinois to exert his influence on the side of his country, and one of the last of his
admonitions to his old political friends, was, that " no man can
be a true Democrat unless he is a loyal patriot." After calling
upon his people to stand by the Constitution and the Union,
Douglas went home and laid down to die.

> "So the struck eagle stretched upon the plain,
> No more through rolling clouds to soar again,
> Viewed his own feather on the fatal dart,
> And winged the shaft that quivered in his heart."

In the death of Douglas the nation lost one of its greatest
and most patriotic men. It is, however, a general law of revolutions, that those who bring them on rarely survive them. But
there is, in the providence of God, a law of compensation that
works a boon to the just and destruction to the vicious. And
in the administration of this compensating law, which works
alike to individuals and to nations, the death of Douglas was
compensated by the gift of Grant to the nation. And in the
providence of God, Gov. Yates was made the commissioner by
whose hands this compensating law was administered, and
Grant, meek and humble, like Jeptha of old, was commissioned
to lead strong men to battle, and soon he proved to be the bold-

est captain in Israel. He moved forward to make battle against the enemies of his country, and no man could do it so well. He smote the enemy hip and thigh. His career was onward and upward, and as the crowning work he led the armies of the Republic to the achievement of the mightiest victory ever won by a military chieftain in the tide of time. In all his services he was the same stern, invincible and original self. He went amid danger and danger fled from his presence. He escaped the assassin's knife when other illustrious men were assaulted and slain. And when the duties of the camp and the cabinet were all discharged, and the Republic redeemed and fixed in history, this silent man, this great captain of our age, unfettered from duty, went forth to make the circuit of nations. He was hailed and honored by the titled dignitaries and the great of all lands. He carried the honor of the young Republic amid the ruins of mighty empires and where kings laid down in state. He wrapped the glory of the Republic around the globe and added new honors to the national life and character, and called the people of all lands to speak the praise of this great republican nation of the world; and this man was the gift of Governor Yates to the nation. Wonderful gift! transcendant man! the world's greatest captain of our age is Ulysses S. Grant.

In the prosecution of the war for the Union, Gov. Yates was in constant requisition, and was almost unceasing in the discharge of his duties. Everywhere that duty called him he hastened. He was earnest and impatient in urging, by tongue or pen, not only his own people, but those of the whole country, to greater deeds of valor and to the achievement of greater victories and more shining honors, and there was no man who surpassed him in earnest and patriotic calls to the people. So well did he discharge his personal and official duties that his name and fame became so deeply rooted in the hearts of the people that his services were solicited in every section of the loyal North, from the Atlantic to the Pacific Ocean. When the duties of the executive office were discharged he repaired to the camp, and from the camp to the hospital, and from the hospital to the political council, and from the political council to the battle field; and thus continued in one constant succession of duties, in which he enlisted his whole soul, mind and strength. His labors were made greater because his great, warm and patriotic heart was enlisted in the cause of his country and in the

welfare of the soldiers whom he had urged to peril their lives
on the battle field. Every official paper issued by Yates, every
letter he wrote and every speech he made contained an earnest
plea for the Union, and as chief executive of the great State of
Illinois Gov. Yates soon became the central figure around which
the loyal people of the great Northwest rallied in defense of the
Union, and thus made strong and great as the chosen leader,
the chief executive of this mighty people, his influence in defense of the Union grew to be invincible and he was called to
labor in every part of the loyal North, from sea to sea.

The unfortunate reverses which followed the Union army in
1862, stimulated those in the North who were opposed to the
war to greater efforts of opposition to the cause of the Union,
and in the hour of greatest peril to the supremacy of the Constitution, the leaders of those in sympathy with secession in-
augurated a movement to re-construct the Union and leave New
England out. In his message to the General Assembly of Illinois, January 5th, 1863, Gov. Yates boldly met this new propo-
sition as another treasonable invasion of the Union of these
States. Said he "I shall always glory in the fact that I belong
to a Republic in the galaxy of whose stars New England is among
the brightest and the best. Palsied be the hand that would
sever the ties which bind the East and the West."

Patriotic and loyal alike to every part of the Union, Gov.
Yates confronted and braved all opposition to the rule of the
Constitution. And well may a defense of New England be re-
corded as one of the greatest contributions to American patriotism. For to turn against that region of our common country,
would be to blow out the great intellectual and moral lights of
the nation and to shut the door of progress against mankind.
New England gave us the spelling book and the dictionary, the
common school system, and inventions in art. No, no! New
England is ours! The continent is ours. It is all ours from
the rising to the setting sun, and from the polar snows to the
warm Gulf that bounds the South and—

"A million hearts shall be riven
Before one golden link is lost."

In all the affairs of life he was the same warm-hearted and
magnanimous man, and from his great sympathetic nature the
love and aspirations of his soul went out to his countrymen, as

virtue went out from that pure, desponding, but celestial man of Nazareth to the wan woman, weak and sick. And with an unbroken record of life, he may well have said with Sir Robert Peel: "It may be that I shall leave a name sometimes to be remembered with expressions of good will in the abodes of those whose lot it is to earn their daily bread by the sweat of their brows, when they shall recruit their exhausted strength with abundant and untaxed food, the sweeter because it is not leavened by a sense of injustice."

Perhaps the boldest official act of Governor Yates was the · prorogation of the Illinois Legislature. The war had been in progress nearly two years. The strength and energy of the loyal people of the nation were brought into requisition by the Washington Government, and still the succession of death and disaster which followed the armies of the Union, spread gloom and doubt over the country. Seeing this terrible condition of things, Abraham Lincoln said, that without the help of the Negro the Union must perish. The Emancipation Proclamation was issued January 1st, 1863. This national edict. this new law from the nation's Sinai, intensified the contest, and made desperation the rule of action for the Confederates. At this time the Legislature of Illinois was in the hands of the Democratic party, and the bitter partisan strife engendered by the war was intensifying political differences between the Democrats and Republicans. The Legislature met January 5th, 1863; and encouraged by the proclamation of emancipation, Governor Yates declared in his annual message, with unusual vigor of speech, his unalterable devotion to the Union and renewed confidence in the success of the armies of the Government. But the dominant party in the Legislature was already well grounded in other views on national affairs than those of Governor Yates, and the session was regarded more as an impediment to the cause of the Union than a support to the loyal soldiers of the State. Thus actuated and thus acting, the Legislature of Illinois became notorious all over the country, and after having extended the session into June, and the two houses failing to agree on a resolution to adjourn, Governor Yates seized his right under the Constitution, and disolved the Legislature by a message of prorogation. Anticipating a disagreement of the Legislature on the subject of adjourning, the Governor prepared his message, and prompt to the time of disagreement, he with his private secretary entered the Representatives' Hall. The Governor took his place, and, with an earnest air of authority, awaited the reading of the message. His private secretary stepped to the Speaker's desk, and promptly announced "a message from the Governor." Anticipating a legal thunderbolt from the Executive, an effort was made to suppress and shut off the reading of the message, but to no avail; an opportunity so important to the cause of the Union was not to be lost by the loyal Governor of Illinois, who stood so high and so near the life of the nation, and in whose charge so great a trust had been committed by the people of this great State.

The message reads as follows:

To the General Assembly of the State of Illinois:

WHEREAS, On the 8th day of June, A. D., 1863, the Senate adopted a joint resolution to adjourn, *sine die* on said day at 7 o'clock p. m., which resolution, upon being submitted, on the same day, to the House of Representatives, was by them amended, by substituting the 22d day of June, and the hour of 12 o'clock, in which amendment, the Senate thereupon refused to concur; and, whereas, the Constitution of this State contains the following provision to-wit:

SEC. 13, ART. 4. In case of a disagreement between the two Houses, with respect to the time of adjournment, the Governor shall have power to adjourn the General Assembly to such a time as he thinks proper, provided it be not to a period beyond the next constitutional meeting of the same.'

And, Whereas, I fully believe that the interests of the people of the State will be best subserved by a speedy adjournment, the past history of the Assembly holding out no reasonable hope of beneficial results to the citizens of the State, or the army in the field, from its further continuance;

Now, therefore, in consideration of the existing disagreement between the two Houses, with respect to the time of adjournment, and by virtue of the power vested in me by the Constitution, as aforesaid, I, Richard Yates, Governor of the State of Illinois, do hereby adjourn the General Assembly, now in session, to the Saturday next preceding the first Monday in January, A. D., 1865.

Given at Springfield, this the 10th day of June, A. D. 1863.

(Signed,)   RICHARD YATES, Governor.

While the message was being read in the House, it was also being read in the Senate, and with the quick and daring skill of a determined surgeon, the work was soon done, and the Legislature adjourned. This act of Governor Yates was heralded over the nation with lightning speed, and every heart was thrilled and strengthened with renewed patriotism.

Yates was justly called the War Governor of Illinois, but equally truly was he the war statesman of Illinois; and whether in proroguing a disloyal Legislature or moving the President to more vehement measures of war, he was never deemed rash, and was never accounted unwise. He was always self-poised and always correct and watchful in the execution of his labors.

Anthropologically considered, Richard Yates was of nervous-sanguine temperament; his organic quality was first rate, but too heavily laden with unfavorable conditions of consanguinity. He was of symmetrical form and superior mold of structure. His head measured 23 $\frac{1}{12}$ inches, which size, combined with the temperament and organic quality, was amply large to govern a nation. The coronal region of his brain was largely developed, which, united with a warm, active temperament, added to him large powers of inspiration and moral greatness.

At the close of his gubernatorial term Richard Yates was elected to the United States Senate as the successor of Douglas. When he entered the Senate he was given the chairmanship of the Committee on Territories.

He had already made himself illustrious while Governor, but as as Senator of the United States he found a great field for the display of his abilities and for the illustration of the soundness of his political views. The sharp contests between rivals of distinguished ability and culture afford greater opportunities for the exhibition and development of principles and powers in men than is afforded in the gubernatorial office.

The functions of the executive being chiefly administration, it is only under extraordinary circumstances that the executive of the State or nation is afforded an opportunity to demonstrate superior statesmanship in the discharge of his official duties. On the other hand the Senate afford sample opportunity for most gifted and comprehensive statesmanship, and especially at the time of revolution in the affairs of government and civilization.

And the Senate proved to be no field of labor in which Mr. Yates shrank from duty, or in which he did not readily enter himself as a ready and able debater. The issue of arms made between contesting powers is always plain and direct, and is settled by the contest in battle. The issues in legislation are quite different, and far more difficult to settle. The reconstruction measures, together with contentions with a President not in harmony with the dominant party, made the labors of the United States Senate quite difficult to dispose of. But on all the great questions touching the fundamental principles of our government Senator Yates proved himself to be equal to any occasion, and even to lead in debate. His speeches on national sovereignty and State rights, on the homestead question, on the subject of equality of human rights before the law, and on building a railway to the Pacific, as well as other leading questions of the day, all demonstrated him to be a man of wide grasp and superior abilities.

If any man hesitates to accord to Richard Yates superior abilities and transcendant eloquence, let me refer such an one to his speech in favor of the conviction of President Johnson. In that speech I will point to eloquence equal to that of Burke in the impeachment of Warren Hastings. I will point to pleading equal to that of William Wirt.

I appeal to a single passage in his senatorial address:

I would do justice, and justice requires conviction; justice to the people whom he has so cruelly wronged. I would be merciful, merciful to the millions whose rights he treacherously asssails by his contempt for law. I would have peace; therefore I vote to remove from office this most pestilent disturber of public peace. I would have prosperity among the people, and confidence restored to capital; therefore I vote to punish him whose turbulance makes capital timid and paralyzes our national industries. I would have economy in the administration of public affairs; therefore I vote to depose the promoter and cause of unheard-of official extravagance. I would have honesty in the collection of the public revenues; therefore I vote to remove this patron of the corruptionists. I would have my Government respected abroad; therefore I vote to punish him who subjects us to dishonor by treating law with contempt. I would inspire respect for law in the youth of the land; I therefore impose its penalties upon the most exalted criminal. I would secure and perpetuate liberty, and I therefore vote to purge the citadel of liberty of him who, through murder succeeded to the chief command and seeks to betray us to the enemy.

I fervently pray that this nation may avoid a repetition of that history, of which apostates and usurpers have desolated nations and enslaved mankind. Let our announcement this day to the President, and all future Presidents and all conspirators against the liberties of this country, be what is already the edict of our land, " You shall not tear this temple of liberty down." Let our warning go down the ages, that every usurper and bold violator of law who thrusts himself in the path of this Republic to honor and renown, whoever he may be, however high his title or proud his name, that, Arnold-like, he shall be gibbetted upon every hill-top throughout the land as a monument of his crime and punishment, and of the shame and grief of his country.

We are not alone in this cause. Out on the Pacific shore a deep murmur is heard from thousands of patriot voices; it swells over the western plain, peopled by millions more; with every increasing volume it advances; on by the lakes, and through the busy marts of the great north, and re-echoed by other millions on the Atlantic strand, it thunders upon us a mighty nation's verdict, *guilty*. While from out of the smoke and gloom of this desolated South, from the rice fields, and along the great rivers, from hundreds of thousands of persecuted and basely betrayed Unionists, comes also the solemn judgment, *guilty*.

In review, in a single word, the life of Richard Yates; he was a child of the wilderness. He was gifted with a bright and shining genius. From boyhood to ripe manhood his career was constantly upward, in the affairs of state and nation. He was a lofty patriot, a hero and benefactor of his age, and his whole life crowned him as a transcendant TRUE MAN, and as such will he be fixed in history. He was brave and demonstrative in the expression of his own views upon all questions of public concern, and with a marked individuality he proclaimed his own convictions, and determined for himself what path of duty he would walk. So decided was he in his own convictions and his own superior selfhood, that when charged in the Senate of following the leadership of Charles Sumner he promptly replied:

" It has been said sarcastically that, upon this question, the Senator from Massachusetts is radical. It is said to me that I follow in the wake of the Senator from Massachusetts. Sir, I do not follow in any man's wake; but I do not object to this accusation. I do not deem it a reproach to be a disciple of that distinguished Senator, the worthy representative of that grand old Commonwealth " where American liberty raised its first voice." For a quarter of a century that Senator has been the fearless champion of human rights. He has occupied the advance guard, the outpost in the army of progress. Triumphant over calumny and unawed by personal violence, with a keen, prophetic eye upon the great result to be attained, with the scimeter of truth and justice in his hand, and the banner of the Union over his head, he has pressed onward to the goal of final victory. Although yet in the vigor of his manhood he has lived to see the small band of pioneers who stood by him swollen to mighty millions. His views have already been embraced and lauded as the wisest statesmanship. They have been written upon the very frontispiece of the age in which he lives; written in the history of the mighty events which are transpiring around us; written in the constitutions and the laws, both national and State, of his country. Where he stood yesterday other statesmen stand to-day. Where he stands in 1868 other statesmen will stand in 1872. Say what we may, there are none in this country who can contest the right of his tall plume to wave at the head of freedom's all-conquering hosts."

Like many other gifted men of our race, he sometimes wandered from the shining path of righteousness, but, as Castelar says of Byron, he was the echo of an uncertain age. His mind was sometimes crossed with sunbeams and shadows, but his life was great and the history of his labors will forever remain a glittering jewel in the aureole of Illinois. And say what you may—

> " In men whom men condemn as ill
> I find so much of goodness still ;
> In men whom men pronounce divine
> I find so much of sin and blot,
> I hesitate to draw the line
> Between the two, where God has not."

The accumulated penalty of a violated law of consanguinity for three generations were transmitted to him. He entered into the conflicts of public life with men, "fierce and vengeful," in struggles of ambition for the ascendancy, and everywhere he was a chosen leader of his people, in proclaiming new political principles and promoting party ascendancy. No man in Illinois was loved so well by his people, and no man loved his people so well as did Richard Yates. He was the embodiment of political progress, and an able exponent of the divine rights of man. I knew him well. I knew his inner life, and there were far greater depths of thought in his soul than belong to the popular and successful politician. But our arbitrary society and civilization hedged him about, and weary to give utterance to the riper and greater thoughts of his mind, he felt disappointed in the great contest and official triumphs in life.

When I behold the innate greatness of this man's soul, and the struggle of his unsatisfied ambition to leap the narrow boundaries of his own intellectual Eden, to pluck and eat new fruit from the tree of knowledge of good and evil, whereby to enter upon higher missions of life and thought and to achieve higher intellectual conquests—I rejoice in his transcendent majesty of mind. The higher thoughts of our race are gleams of intellectual light flashing from the far-off millennium upon the loftiest intellects of our way-wandering age. The flash not rarely is disastrous to the favored mind. While it illuminates, so it sometimes consumes. Such was the mournful fate of Kirk White, of Keats, of Pollock. Such was the fate of Yates—of whom we may say:

> " 'T was thine own genius gave the fatal blow,
> And helped to plant the dart that laid thee low."

Although a political reformer, Richard Yates was highly endowed with a wise conservatism, which gives revolutionary thought the semblance of moderation. He was keenly sensible of the influence of new political thought on the public mind, and in entering upon a great contest he fully comprehended the obstacles of ignorance, prejudice and institutionalism to be encountered.

In public life, no man was more free from mistakes than Richard Yates. So well and wisely were all his acts and movements directed in party politics and in the discharge of official duties, that it almost seemed as though he could not commit a blunder against his party and against the public interest. And no man throughout this vast country was ever more endeared to his people than was Richard Yates. Gen. Jackson had ardent admirers and bitter enemies; Henry Clay was idolized by political friends and personal admirers; strong attachments existed between William H. Seward and his constituents; and in like manner was Senator Douglas endeared to his friends. But there never existed that warm, pliant, filial love between either of these eminent men and the people such as existed between Yates and the people of Illinois. He was the adored and loving patriot of this Commonwealth. He was the embodiment of high, manly qualities with an individuality endowed of divine gifts. He possessed the heroism of the warrior, and the delicately attuned nature of the babe Christabel.

The following beautiful tribute ,to the American Volunteer, fully attests his refined sensibilities :

The name or title of the " American Volunteer " is illustrious with all that is good, and noble, and great. Around that simple name clusters all that is glorious in devotion to country, all that is precious or dear in liberty, all that is grand in lofty prowess, and all that is sublime in brilliant achievements. No hero of antiquity, no soldier in modern warfare, ever scaled such a shining summit of human fame as the " American Volunteer." He made the name of the Republic a triumph and a joy at home and in foreign lands. He fought against secession, slavery, and barbarism for a higher civilization, for progress, the Union of the States, for the life of the nation, and to establish upon solid and enduring foundations the equal rights, liberty, and happiness of all the children of God. He placed the capstone upon the temple of liberty, which our fathers had built, and consecrated it to the freedom and enfranchisement of all men, without regard to caste. The " American Volunteer," though he may now sleep in the lowly tenements of clay, speaks through history way down the coming centuries, and says to all succeeding generations as the nation grows in power and grandeur with her institutions, the noblest and freest, her civilization the highest and the purest, and her flag, the most honored of the world, " This nation, these institutions, this civilization, and that flag are mine, for I fought and died to secure them to me and you, and your and my posterity forever."

What pen could portray the disaster, the ruin, and the death which would have covered this land, if our enemies had consummated the traitor schemes of discord and disunion? The answer to this question shows, in some measure, the immense debt of gratitude we owe the 300,000 brave and gallant spirits, who sealed their devotion to liberty and to the nation with their precious blood.

Oh! what a sacrifice was there, my countrymen, on the altar of patriotic duty. Three hundred thousand bloody shrouds pass in long ghastly procession before us. There rises up before us 500 battle fields strewn with the dead, the wounded, and the dying, and a million of "bosoms bared to whatever of terror there may be in war and death." All these we have seen, but thanks be to our dead and living soldiers, all now is peace, and we shall see them no more. And here was also the sacrifice, not only of life, but of affection. The father willingly gave up his son to his country's service, though he knew he might return lame, maimed or wounded—without a leg or an arm—or never returning, sleep the sleep of death, in an unknown grave, in a far off land. The widowed mother, in many thousands of instances, gave up all her sons, or her only son; the farmer and mechanic sent their sons forth, and vacant places have been made at the hearthstone of almost every Northern loyal household, that the life of the Republic might be saved. It was the sacrifice of affection, for if there is one tie stronger than another, it is the tie that binds the devoted wife to the husband—how strong the tie "in the hidden soul of sympathy," which binds the father to his boy, and who can fathom the ocean depth of a mother's love?

Go to that little cabin by the brook, or on the hillside, and see the fond wife or fond mother, standing in the doorway, and, with blinding tears, bidding adieu to all she has or loves on earth. We see the husband or son on their winding way—

> "Upon the hill they turn to take
> A last fond look
> Of the valley and the village church,
> And the cottage by the brook."

Alas! when that wife and mother stood in the doorway watching the return of the army, how her cheek turned pale. Alas! the face of that bright-eyed boy lies pale in death, and that husband never more shall return.

> "Alas! nor wife, nor children more shall he behold,
> Nor friends, nor sacred home."

Far off on the banks of Southern rivers, on many a hillside, or in valleys low, in many a sequestered nook, in narrow little tenements, repose the bones of our noble dead No kind wife, mother or sister there to console the spirit as it passed the boundary stream of life; no friendly hand to strew flowers on his grave.

> "He sleeps his last sleep; he has fought his last battle,
> No sound shall awake him to glory again."

But he died for his country. He has gone but a little while before us; we may not fill as honorable graves.

His name shall never be forgot
While fame her record keeps,
And Glory points the hallowed spot
Where Valor proudly sleeps.''

In his nobler manhood he walked the royal way of life; he taught his fellows higher principles of political society and more royal lessons of patriotism. He was true to the living, and in his death, let it be the ambition and the duty of the living to be true to him. Let the people of Illinois not forget him who stood at the helm of State four long, weary and eventful years, watching and pleading for the life of the Republic. His name was a tower of strength in that awful time of the nation's greatest tragedy and transition. His name strengthened the weak and gave greater confidence to the strong. At his pleadings mighty armies were encouraged to do battle. At the cry of the widow and the wounded soldier, his ear caught the sound, and the State of Illinois responded to the supplicant. He was a gifted patriot, a grand man, and a great benefactor. Let not the people of Illinois forget this man who gave the measure of his life to the cause of his State and his country. Then, let me implore you, people of Illinois to not forget the shining deeds of your dead statesman.

" Then build for him the marble shrine,
Pure as his patriot soul is shriven ;
On it let treasures be bestowed
Freely as was his life-work given ;
That in the better coming time
Our country, joined by bands fraternal,
May not forget his deeds sublime,
But keep them ever fresh and vernal."

All the great periods, epochs, and events in the world's history, are inscribed with great endeavor to advance the intellectual and moral progress of mankind, and the boldest in thought, of the men and women of our race have learned with Castelar, that inspired Spaniard, that ". Life is full of complications, and for the same reason, of insuperable difficulties. And as there are great contrasts in nature, there are also in society opposing forces. By the side of the prophet who announces the future, arises the magistrate who believes his mission to be the conservation of the present system, and who as a result of this conviction, persecutes the prophet. In the vicinity of every new thinker, there exists an association which believes itself infallible. Beside each reformer is placed the eternal cup of hemlock. We can not aspire to be blessed by posterity, without being cursed by our cotemporaries."

The pressure and power of old institutions has often caused many a good genius to fail and fall by the wayside of life, who otherwise would have been a benefactor of mankind.

The greatest impediment to human progress existing in our age, is the dogma of infallibility ; and in saying this, I do not refer wholly to the infallibility of the Romish Pontiff, for that is of little concern to the enlightened, intellectual mass of mankind, but I refer in a broader sense to the doctrine of the eternal finality of creeds and institutions; to that high wall, that fortress of incrusted institutionalism, that barricades all our centers of learning against the dawning intellectual and religious light of coming ages.

Intellectual and moral institutions established for the dissemination of knowledge among men, without the function of inspiration to light the way of the human mind to other and unknown fields of knowledge, are organized intellectual and moral despotisms. In such institutions is enthrowned intellectual and moral power, and that power shuts the door against the onward progress of the human soul.

We build our highest and most sacred monuments to genius and religion, on the hopes of the future, but we shut the windows of our souls against the prophecies of the intellectual light of the future. No wonder our age is not better. We have built our cities of civilization on the ruins of the villages of the aborigines, and our institutions of learning are, to a great extent, founded on the thoughts of Pagan institutions. Our civilization is founded upon individualism — a system of society that requires locks on the doors of the houses in which we live, and a strong police force, to make honesty the best policy. Individualism is an incidental condition in the social order, and not an enduring form of society. It is the doctrine of the big fish eating up the little fish ; a system admirably adapted to the present progressive condition of the human mind, and of the civil rights of the people. In olden times, the rulers of the people absorbed the earnings and happiness of their subjects. The order is now changed, and the rulers and teachers have constructed a system of society and government that allows the strong and the crafty to absorb the earnings and happiness of the people. Such a system of society builds palaces for idiots, and in which they are fed on the fat of the land, while philosophers and reformers are left to starve in hovels and garrets, while the teachers of religion and science devote most of their spare time to the reading of novels. And this condition of society exists under the Christian dispensation and under the reign of the higher law. And if men " do these things in the green tree what shall be done in the dry? "

We have had amendments to the Constitution designed to perfect our political society. I am in favor of an amendment to the Declaration of Independence, and also to the Golden Rule, to point the way to perfecting our social order, and promoting human happiness. Let us henceforth learn that we hold these truths to be self-evident that all men are entitled to happiness in political society. Aye, more than this, let us henceforth teach whatsoever the citizen owes to society, that, also, does society owe unto the citizen. Let us strike for these high achievements in social and political society and henceforth the fruits of our revolutions of arms and ideas will be far more perfect, and human happiness become far more general to the human race, to the end that a righteous proletarianism will so unite the individual life with the public life, as to unfold a law of universal attraction, for the government and guidance of the great whole.

> " Then peace on earth will hold her easy sway,
> And man forget his brother man to slay,
> And milder arts will martial arts succeed,
> And both will march to gain the immortal meed."

There is a deeper lesson to be learned from the great conflict of the Civil War than the victories of mighty armies can teach, than the defeat of brave men can suggest. It is the lesson that grows out of our humanity and with the voice of inspiration speaking back from more golden ages of the future, and testified to by the risen patriots from their immortal homes above, that we are entering an elevated plane of intellectual and moral life, which will bind our common humanity together in one fraternity, until peace and righteousness will so pervade the whole that there will be no Lost Causes, no fallen foes, no boasted victories over kindred slain, to mar the divine adminis-

tration of universal law alike to each member of our great
national family.

Like Daniel Manin, Richard Yates died away from home.
But, as in the fulness of time the remains of Manin were taken
from the world's city of civilization, with an escort composed
of the gifted of the press, and transferred through the defiles
of the Alps, and through rich and gorgeous lands and national-
ities, to be restored to mother earth, in the bosom of his home,
amid the courtly grandeur of the fair metropolis of the Adri-
atic, so was the dead statesman of Illinois returned to his
final resting-place, in the bosom of his long-loved home. With
solemn obsequies, and the benedictions of friends and patriots,
he was transferred, with full rank and title, to the grand army
of the heroic dead. And thus another name of those

" Gone up from every land to people heaven."

was added; another star was placed in the pantheon of the
world's political progress; and as I turn to behold the name
of Richard Yates fixed in history as one of the evangels of
human liberty, whose principles have been enacted into the
statutes of the nation, and whose deeds have added lustre to
its fame, I catch the inspiration of his great soul flashing down
from the eternal world. Looking down through the generations which are to follow. I see the political principles in defense
of which he gave the full measure of his services, rooted in the
national life, growing and fruiting in the hearts of the people,
until the divine idea is consummated in this new world by the
supremacy of the American Constitution over the entire continent; and I see the stars above vieing with the stars below,
to establish for the future millions of this people one home,
one language, one law, and one faith -- to the end that it may
be one and supreme among nations in grandeur and in righteousness.

www.ingramcontent.com/pod-product-compliance
Lightning Source LLC
Chambersburg PA
CBHW031221290326
41931CB00036B/1330